Why Is A Stepfather Called A Stepfather?

A Tribute To Good Stepfathers

By

J. F. McCormick, III

authorHOUSE™

1663 LIBERTY DRIVE, SUITE 200
BLOOMINGTON, INDIANA 47403
(800) 839-8640
WWW.AUTHORHOUSE.COM

First published by AuthorHouse 03/15/05

ISBN: 1-4208-2874-6 (e)
ISBN: 1-4208-2875-4 (sc)

Printed in the United States of America
Bloomington, Indiana

This book is printed on acid-free paper.

Table of Contents

Step
'1'
"If I Perish, I Perish"

All of us are probably somewhat familiar with the story in the book of Esther that so beautifully illustrates God's providence for believers as He works behind the scenes unbeknownst to us, in order to bring about the deliverance of His people. A people I might add, who were facing sure extermination at the hand of the their captors, the Babylonians.

If you're in a place where it seems like every weapon of Satan's arsenal is loaded, locked, and ready to fire upon you, and all that you can think of is "Woe Is Me", please take time to read the book of Esther.

If you want drama, it's there. If you want mystery, it's there. If you want suspense, it's there. If you want the unexpected, expect it in the Book of Esther.

What can be more dramatic than a woman who is a slave ending up as the Queen of Babylon? What can be more mysterious and suspenseful than her king not knowing that she is a Jew as he orders all the Jews to be put to death? What can be more unexpected than a man being hang on the very gallows that he built to hang his Jewish archenemy on?

One of the greatest blessings that I received from the story of Esther is the fact that God is forever (like 24 & 7 forever) interceding on behalf of His people. And guess what? This divine intercession on our behalf usually takes place behind the scenes, which means, at any given moment when we think that He is unaware or even unconcerned, He is aware and He is concerned! So regardless of what things look like, taste like, smell like, feel like, or sound like, God promises to never leave nor forsake us if we don't leave nor forsake Him. This sounds like a great deal to me!

I believe that your faith will increase in leaps and bounds as you see God working in every way conceivable in order to deliver the nation of Israel from the hand of the enemy. The main character who played a great part in this deliverance of a nation was Esther.

The highpoint of this story came when Esther said, *"...so will I go in unto the King which is not according unto the law: and if I perish, I perish"* (Esther 4:16). Esther spoke these words as she prepared to go before the king in an attempt to bring about the deliverance of her people. So why was her life at stake? Why? Her life was at stake because no

2

one was allowed to go before the king unless he sent forth a personal invitation requesting their presence.

Now even though Esther was his queen, this rule applied to her as well as to everyone else. Nevertheless, Esther went before the king without being summoned and God gave her favor as the king allowed her to approach him, and the rest is history! Justice was done! Israel was saved! God was glorified!

Step

'2'

Mordecai, A Good Stepfather!

A few years ago as Father's Day approached, I fasted and prayed asking the Lord to give me something different to minister that would bless fathers. Over the years, I ministered several Father's Day messages like *"Fathers! The Good, the Bad, and the Ugly"* and *"Fathers, Husbands, and Men."* The latter message stressed the importance of developing relationships according to God's order of things. Fathers, husbands, and men is the way that many men enter into relationships today. They father a baby first, then may become a husband to their baby's mother, and many very seldom become the men that God created them to be! God's order of things goes like this: Be a man first by keeping yourself sexually pure until you become a husband. Then, be fruitful and multiply by becoming a father. So there you have it, men, husbands, and fathers! That's God's order of things. I had these messages and many more, but I felt the need for a fresh and different message.

I recall asking the Lord to give me something straight from His heart. A short time afterwards, I felt led to minister on the subject of good stepfathers. Needless to say, when the thought of ministering to stepfathers on Father's Day came to my mind, I had no precedence as far as putting the message together. In other words, as far as I could remember, I couldn't recall hearing a message aimed at revealing the utmost importance of good stepfathers. That's why I thank God for the Holy Spirit. Why? I thank Him because He led me to the Book of Esther, chapter 2:

> Est 2:5 Now in Shushan the palace there was a certain Jew, whose name *was* Mordecai, the son of Jair, the son of Shimei, the son of Kish, a Benjamite;
>
> Est 2:6 Who had been carried away from Jerusalem with the captivity which had been carried away with Jeconiah king of Judah, whom Nebuchadnezzar the king of Babylon had carried away.
>
> Est 2:7 And he brought up Hadassah, that is, Esther, his uncle's daughter: for she had neither father nor mother, and the maid *was* fair and beautiful; whom Mordecai, when her father and mother were dead, took for his own daughter.

We see here that the inhabitants of Judah had been defeated by King Nebuchadnezzar and carried off to Babylon as slaves. Among those captured was a Jewish man by the name of Mordecai. Verse 7 tells us that Mordecai brought up a Jewish girl by the name of Hadassah, that is, Esther. Esther's parents were deceased, so Mordecai took Esther for his own daughter. So in a sense, Mordecai became to Esther what we today would call a stepfather.

When I mention the word stepfather, I'm sure various thoughts begin to circulate within a lot of people's minds. And guess what? By reason of the epidemic number of stepfather situations that turn sour, many of those thoughts are unpleasant to say the least. There are countless stories of stepfathers not only mentally and physically abusing their stepchildren, but many times these men abuse the children's mother also. I've heard of accounts of stepchildren who spoke about their growing up with seven different stepfathers and their being abused by all of them!

That is why we will place our main focus upon this good man whose name is Mordecai. I refer to him as a good man because it was out of the true sincere goodness of his heart that he took it upon himself to raise up another man's daughter as if she was his own flesh and blood. There are countless good stepfathers who are doing this same thing right now today. So as we look at Mordecai, let's see if we can figure out why stepfathers are called stepfathers.

Step
'3'
Mordecai Stepped In

At verse 7 of Esther chapter 2, we see that there came a time when Esther's mother and father were no longer able to love her anymore. A time when they were no longer able to care for her, nurture her, or continue rearing her anymore. It was then that Mordecai stepped in as a father to do these things for Esther. Maybe that's one reason why a stepfather is called a stepfather. The King James Version says Mordecai took Esther "for his own daughter." Say it with me, "for his own daughter."

Don't miss this people! I believe that God placed these words here for a specific reason. Say it with me again, "for his own daughter." Once again please, "for his own daughter." I need to pause here and say this concerning this statement of God, "for his own daughter". It's distressing to say, but right now today, far too many men step into marriages with bad intentions instead of good intentions. Unfortunately, many times when there are daughters in that fatherless home that are "fair and beautiful" as verse 7 says Esther was, these want-to-be stepfathers have no intention of loving and caring for these "fair and beautiful" daughters as if they were their own biological daughters! Instead, these men, who are nothing like the good man Mordecai, desire to step into these marriages because they have eyes for those "fair and beautiful" daughters! This is why they are anxious to step in! Hello Somebody! However, Mordecai stepped into the extended role of stepfather to love and to nurture Esther as though she was his own flesh and blood daughter. What I'm talking about is the love of a good stepfather. On the one hand, I believe that God spoke these four words, "for his own daughter", in order to let us know that it's easy for us and it's expected of us to love, to nurture, to care for, to comfort, to pity, to be merciful to, to be proud of, and to work through blood, sweat and tears, for those who are our own. While on the other hand, when it comes to doing all of these things and more for children who are not our own biological children, of whom we can't sit around and look at them and see that they have our eyes, ears, nose, lips, or other inherited traits… When a father can't sit around and see these things in the children that he is raising, it's not so easy. And guess what? That's why it takes an exceptional man with an exceptional heart of love to step into an exceptional situation like this, and give his lifelong commitment to do all of these things for children that are not his biological sons and daughters. Again, maybe that's why they call a stepfather a stepfather!

I believe that God wants us to know that He loves good stepfathers with a special kind of love. Why? Because in His sight, they may be the most special kind of fathers that there are. This is in no way saying that God is a respecter of persons. This is in no way saying that fathers who are still in the home raising their biological children are not special to God. However, what I feel God was saying is this: "Whatever it takes to be considered as a great natural father, it takes a great deal more just to be considered a good stepfather!" In other words, it seems as though, in order for a stepfather to be considered just plain old vanilla good, he has to do far more than a biological father does. He has to put up with far more than a biological father puts up with. He has to take far more than a biological father takes in the family setting.

It's like there is one set of normal standards for the biological father and another set for the stepfather that are abnormal in the sense of what is required of him by his new wife and his stepchild in order for him to be accepted.

Step

'4'

It's Natural To Love Our Own

Did you know that God created mankind in a special way that causes us to be proud of people, places and things that are our own? If you don't believe me, how many of you who are reading any one of the millions of copies of this book right now (speaking by faith), are more proud of someone else's children than you are of your own? How many of you are more proud of someone else's possessions more than you are of your own possessions? Naturally speaking, we're proud of the accomplishments of other people's children, but we are more proud when our children accomplish the same things. Naturally speaking, this is not bad. Naturally speaking, this is natural! Why? Because this is the way God created us as human beings.

Now you don't have to tell me, but in this day and time, there are so many Bible toting, scripture quoting, devil smoting, huge cross hanging around their neck believers (much like myself), that someone may be saying, "Pastor, wait just a minute here now! That sounds mighty selfish to me. Being a Pastor, I'm sure that you're aware that the Bible says selfishness is a sin in the sight of God. What say ye to these things, Pastor?"

"So," says the Pastor, "the $100,000 question is, are we really guilty of being selfish when we are more committed, more dedicated, more loving, more caring, and more willing to sacrifice when it comes to those who are our own? Or, is this natural to us as humans?" Check this out.

> 1Ti 5:8 But if any provide not for his own, and specially for those of his own house, he hath denied the faith, and is worse than an infidel.

Judging by this, it seems as though to a great degree, God Himself expects us to do for our own even at the neglect of doing for those who are not our own. So when a man steps in and takes on the exceptional responsibility of being a good stepfather, many times those things which are natural must be placed aside. He must now become willing to walk no more in certain natural areas that are comfortable to him, but rather, he must now become willing to walk in areas that require him to do the unnatural, and do it well.

Now for those who believe that it's a piece of cake for a person to ignore the natural and flawlessly flow in the unnatural as far as stepfathers are concerned, please answer these questions: Is it easy for a leopard to change its spots? Is it easy for a tiger to change its stripes? Of course the obvious answer to both of these questions is: It's impossible for a leopard or a tiger to change their natural makeup. But guess what? When it comes to man it's different. Why is it different for man?

> 1Co 15:38 But God giveth it a body as it hath pleased him, and to every seed his own body.

> 1Co 15:39 All flesh is not the same flesh: but there is one kind of flesh of men, another flesh of beasts, another of fishes, and another of birds.

So even though flesh is flesh, all flesh does not possess the same attributes. As we look at the different kinds of flesh listed in the above scripture, we need to recognize that the more superior flesh or the more excellent flesh is that of man. Why? Well, let's allow the book of Genesis to answer that for us.

> Gen 1:24 And God said, Let the earth bring forth the living creature after his kind, cattle, and creeping thing, and beast of the earth after his kind: and it was so.

> Gen 1:26 And God said, Let us make man in our image, after our likeness: and let them have dominion over the fish of the sea, and over the fowl of the air, and over the cattle, and over all the earth, and over every creeping thing that creepeth upon the earth.

> Gen 1:27 So God created man in his *own* image, in the image of God created he him; male and female created he them.

> Gen 1:28 And God blessed them, and God said unto them, Be fruitful, and multiply, and replenish the earth, and subdue it: and have dominion over the fish of the sea, and over the fowl of the air, and over every living thing that moveth upon the earth.

So we see at verse 24 that God is going about the business of creating flesh upon the earth. He created cattle, creeping things, and the beast of the earth. These animals were ordained by God to reproduce after their own kind. In other words, they could only produce the same type of flesh that they were made of. Then at verse 26 we see that God made man in His image and His likeness.

Now without getting too technical, this is what the deal is concerning the flesh of man as compared to the flesh of animals in this Earth realm. On the one hand, man is made in the image and the likeness of God which enables him to operate in a way that goes beyond the natural and into the unnatural, and even into the supernatural! While on the other hand, those in the animal kingdom are bound to operating according to the laws of nature only. Lastly, at verse 26, we see God giving man dominion over all the other flesh that He had created upon the Earth. This can be interpreted as God's declaration that the flesh of man is the more superior and the more excellent flesh upon the Earth.

Step

'5'

Lions Refuse To Be Stepfathers

When I was a young(er) man, like just about everybody else, I had a few convictions. I loved music and had accumulated over three hundred records. Even though I really loved music, I had one conviction that I usually stuck to. When a band released their new album, I would go to the record store and read the list of songs on the cover. If I saw an old song that had been released by another group in times past, usually I wouldn't purchase the album. Why? Because when I purchased a new album I wanted to hear all new material! I wanted my monies worth.

I also had a conviction concerning movies. It was not a part of my natural way of thinking that I would pay to see a movie if it was a cartoon. I guess I didn't think it was worth it to pay "x" amount of dollars to see a movie of which the producers didn't have to pay real live actors to star in! On the one hand, I can see paying $5, $6, or $7 to see a movie that featured a famous actor or actress. After all, these people don't come cheap. On the other hand, my conviction kicked in saying, "Why should you pay the same kind of money to see a movie whose main star is nothing but ink animated on paper?"

Now as I got older, my wife and I were blessed to birth three children, two girls and an only begotten son. As they grew up, it was at this time that I was finally forced to pay hard earned money to see a movie that was created with cartoon characters. The movie was *The Lion King*. In retrospect, I must admit that I didn't want to go see the movie, and it showed in my attitude. But guess what? The movie was not only excellent, but I came dangerously close to shedding some alligator tears because of the humane story line and the touching plot! Yes Sir, those lions taught me something that's for sure. So there went one conviction down the drain.

While we are speaking of lions, what actually happens in the wild can serve as a great example of what I mentioned earlier. Do you recall when I spoke about how unnatural and how difficult it can be for a man to take on the responsibility of accepting another man's children as if they were his own? Well, check this out. In basically every pride of lions, there are usually males, females, and cubs. Now even though this sounds like a "Home Sweet Home" kind of a setup, what happens regularly is very traumatic for the lionesses and her cubs when their pride is taken over by males other than the ones that fathered their cubs.

When male cubs are born into the pride, they can only remain with the pride until they become sexually mature, which usually takes from two to three years. When they reach this age, the fathers of the young male lions force their sons to leave the pride and they must now set out to mark their own territory and establish their own pride. During this same time, the lionesses and other suckling cubs remain with the pride.

So where is the best place for these young testosterone filled male lions to find themselves a little honey of a lioness for their mate? Where else, but in the midst of some other pride out in the wild that has just kicked out a group of young males much like themselves? These banished males can only possess a pride of females for a few years because after then, they will have reached the age that would render them incapable of defending the pride against other incoming younger males. So needless to say, when the young male lions locate a pride with an ample supply of lionesses, their first priority is to get on with the dating game. Now even though this is the natural thing for them to do, many times the females still have cubs from the former pride of males, and if these cubs are still suckling cubs, most lionesses are not fertile and cannot mate at that particular time. Now it's like, "Houston, we have a problem!"

Well, exactly what is the problem? If these young males were to wait until the suckling cubs were old enough to no longer depend upon mama for their nourishment, it may be too late for them to father enough cubs to make sure that their generation will continue into the next.

Let's pause right about here for station identification if you will. Earlier I tried to bring home the point about the impossibility of a leopard changing its spots and of a tiger changing its stripes. Let's add to that list the impossibility of a lion changing its natural mating habits. I say this because of what the incoming male lions do in order to guarantee that the female lions with cubs are able to mate at the time of their entrance into the new pride.

Since the presence of suckling cubs causes the female lion to be unable to mate, the new males begin to search the surrounding area for her hidden cubs. When they are found, the young male lions kill them off one by one! Now even though there were a few violent scenes in the movie, *The Lion King*, they didn't reveal this aspect of life within a pride of lions in the wild. But as tragic as it sounds, this is a drama that repeats itself over and over throughout the ages.

A short time after this slaughter of the lion cubs, the used to be mother lionesses can be found flirting with the new male who had brutally killed her cubs! I'm sure that to many people and probably to many lions also, this seems to be unethical and just plain old wrong! Like, something is definitely wrong with this picture! Nevertheless, the lionesses have no other choice because it is the natural thing for them to do.

So it is evident that many in the animal kingdom can't go for this stepfather business! That's why I say, when it concerns mankind, it takes an exceptional man to step in and care for another man's child as though he or she were his own. You know, we may be getting somewhere as we try to figure out exactly why we call a stepfather a stepfather!

Step
'6'
How Appreciated Is The Good Stepfather?

Now since this is the way that it is with a good stepfather, being an exceptional man with an exceptional love, who's more than willing to make exceptional sacrifices and more than willing to step into a family situation that has a husbandless mother and a fatherless child, I am sure and very sure that the good stepfather must be highly appreciated by society. And guess what? This appreciation most definitely should come from the mother of whom he has married and also by the child of whom he has taken as his own child just as Mordecai did with Esther.

Now if you're anything like the average person, then you are a person of compassion as well as a person who believes in fair play. With this being the case, you are probably one of the ones who think that there is definitely something wrong with the picture of the female lioness going about seeking the attention and the affection of the male lion that just killed her cubs. Paramount to all of this, you will most definitely be one of the ones who thinks that there is definitely something wrong with the picture of a mother and her child not highly appreciating the good husband and the good stepfather who is a part of their lives. Are you with me?

Well, I am a Pastor who has been in the business of the Lord long enough to witness the condition of the above average family whose head is a stepfather. This includes Christian and non-Christian families. I have found that the vast majority of good stepfathers are not having rendered unto them the respect that is due them. No, not by a long shot! Not by society, and worse yet, not by his wife or her child of whom he has taken as if he or she were his biological child. Now this is by no means to say that this is the way that it is with every good stepfather, but I have found that this is the way that it is in far too many cases.

Before we proceed any further, let me share with you something that the Lord dropped into my spirit concerning good stepfathers. I believe the Lord said, "Pastor, I want you to share what I feel about good stepfathers. I want you to teach and preach it straight from My heart to their hearts. I want you to reveal what I feel. I want you to play it the way I say it. I want you to tell it the way that I spell it. I want you to teach and preach it so that they can reach it. But Pastor, please make sure that you make it so that they can take it."

When God spoke these things to me, I knew from past experience that I was about to be put in the same place that the Apostle Paul was put in concerning a group of believers in Corinth:

> 2Co 7:8 I know I distressed you greatly with my letter. Although I felt awful at the time, I don't feel at all bad now that I see how it turned out. The letter upset you, but only for a while.
>
> 2Co 7:9 Now I'm glad--not that you were upset, but that you were jarred into turning things around. You let the distress bring you to God, not drive you from him. The result was all gain, no loss.
>
> 2Co 7:10 Distress that drives us to God does that. It turns us around. It gets us back in the way of salvation. We never regret that kind of pain. But those who let distress drive them away from God are full of regrets, end up on a deathbed of regrets.
>
> 2Co 7:11 And now, isn't it wonderful all the ways in which this distress has goaded you closer to God? You're more alive, more concerned, more sensitive, more reverent, more human, more passionate, more responsible. Looked at from any angle, you've come out of this with purity of heart.

So some mothers along with their children will be challenged from here on out and you may get a little angry. But if your anger drives you closer to God, you nor I will never regret it.

a chance that they may lose them in the process of sharing them. Are you with me? One of those very personal things that men most definitely don't want to share is their wife! Can I get an amen, men? And all the men say, "Amen, Pastor!"

Let the man break it on down for you. It's like the good stepfather is saying, "Oh yeah, I know that she belonged to him a long time ago, but she belongs to me now! So I don't like the idea of her having to be around him because there still may be an outside chance that she may still care for him in some way, or vice versa. Now don't get me wrong, it's not that I don't trust my wife, I just don't trust the situation! You see, as long as her former lover or husband is out of sight, it seems as though he is out of mind. That is the way I would like for him to be! Out of sight and out of mind!" I believe somebody out there can feel me on this one. Am I right?

Nevertheless, all of this aside, a good stepfather realizes that this is something that must be dealt with not in the natural but in the more than natural. What I'm saying is, the good stepfather knows that he must share his wife and stepchild with someone who, in many cases, didn't really care for them like he should have. Besides this, the good stepfather has to live with the pressure of the possibility of losing custody of the child of whom he loves as if he or she was his own son or daughter. How many men are willing to step into a relationship where there has been a bitter divorce? One in which there remains a lot of hard feelings between the two separated parties? One that resembles a war zone at times? One wherein the good stepfather defends and protects his wife and his stepchild, but somehow he ends up being the outside man when his wife, her "ex", and her child begin to triple tag team against him?

This reminds me of something that happens many times when a police officer responds to a domestic disturbance between couples, whether they are married or just shacking. When they arrive at the scene, the embattled couple is getting busy throwing blows. Let's say the woman is receiving the worse blows and she's crying out for help. So naturally, the officer engages the man and in the process the man is now the one who is taking a whipping. To the police officer's amazement, the woman begins to attack him because he is hurting her husband or her man! Countless good stepfathers find themselves in very similar circumstances when those of whom he is defending turn and attack him. These attacks can be mental, verbal, or actual physical attacks.

How many men are willing to step into a situation like this when they have other choices that contain far less drama? I don't mean to sound redundant, but maybe that's why a stepfather is called a stepfather. Here's a question for you. Are you one of the ones who feels like there is something wrong with this picture so far? Wrong in respect to the honor and the esteem that a good stepfather deserves but rarely receives? Wait a minute, there is more. Check out these words of Jesus:

> Mat 10:34 Think not that I am come to send peace on earth: I came not to send peace, but a sword.
>
> Mat 10:35 For I am come to set a man at variance against his father, and the daughter against her mother, and the daughter in law against her mother in law.
>
> Mat 10:36 And a man's foes shall be they of his own household.

That's puzzling! Why would the Prince of Peace say that He did not come to bring peace? Answer: The Jews believed that the Messiah would usher in great outward peace and prosperity, which would have been O.K. if this were indeed the case, but it wasn't. Please don't be confused, because Christ did come to be a peacemaker between God and sinners. Rest assured also that by the blood of His cross, He was the author of spiritual peace to His people. Praises be to God too that the Gospel Christ brought with Him was the Gospel of peace. But in spite of all this, Christ said that He came to tear up families!

Without biting His tongue Christ declared that He came to cause members of the same household to become enemies! Are you confused? Well, you shouldn't be. Why? This is why. What Christ desired His people to know then and now can be summed up as such. Yes, I am the Prince of Peace, wielding the great Gospel of Peace. Translated, this means if any man, woman, boy or girl of any given household choose to submit themselves to Me and My Gospel truth, they will automatically become the enemy of any man, woman, boy or girl in that same household who chooses not to do the same! "That's why I came," declares Christ. In other words, the reason why people living in the same house can become enemies is because of one choosing to stand for what is right, while another chooses to stand for what is wrong.

I was stunned when I read an article once that revealed the number of Pastors who end up walking away from their pastorate because of burnout. Something that Popeye says before he pops the top on a can of spinach explains the feelings of these men of God. Popeye used to say, "I've had all that I can stand and I can't stand no more!" The article revealed that one of the main reasons why they walked away from ministry was not because of the periodic, clockwork-like pressure that comes along with the territory of being a God-called, God-ruled Pastor. Truth be told, the straw that broke the backs of many of these Pastors came in the form of the pressure they came home to, that was the same kind of pressure that they had to battle on a regular basis within the ministry. This is when the pressure became extraordinary in its scope. What I'm saying is, in any given ministry, on any given Sunday, those who choose to do wrong within the confines of the church and don't want to be corrected will consider the Pastor the enemy when he decides to discipline them. Many times, when this disciplinary action is administered, members tend to choose sides. Some support the Pastor's actions while others support the one on the receiving end of the discipline, who usually proceeds to do everything they can in order to discredit the Pastor and hereby credit themselves. The more popular the person is who's in the wrong, the greater chance there is for the Pastor to be considered as the enemy who must be treated as such. Even though this is discouraging, what's even more discouraging is the fact that some of those who were previously praising the Pastor are now a part of the lynch mob crying, "Crucify him!" All of a sudden, it becomes crystal clear what Jesus meant when He said, *"...arm yourselves likewise"* (1 Pet 4:1).

So when the pressure from without is equaled or surpassed by the pressure from within, the combined pressure can easily become extraordinary pressure. It was the opinion of some Pastors who quit that regardless of the pressure of ministry, if their home was a "Home Sweet Home," they could have borne the pressures of ministry. Unfortunately, the overall atmosphere within their home was like the one described by Jesus when He said, *"And a man's foes shall be those of his own household"* (Mt. 10:36).

Step
'8'
The Good Stepfather As The Enemy

It's one thing to be considered the enemy by those outside of the home, but when you're treated like an enemy from those at your own dinner table the pressure can become almost unbearable to many people. It has been my experience that a good percentage of good stepfathers end up as the enemy in their own household. I'm talking about him becoming the enemy among those of whom he is bringing up, feeding, and maintaining.

For those who are wondering how something like this can happen within a household, here's how. In order for enemy situations to come about there has to be opposition between two or more people or between dissenting groups of people. Of course, we all know that wherever there is opposition, hostilities are not too far behind. Sometimes the volatile situation continues to fester without remedy even though one person or one group can be proven more or less to be in the right, while the other can be proven more or less to be wrong. So what is it that's going down in many family settings that has caused, and is still causing, many good stepfathers to become the enemy who is pitted against his wife and her child of which he has taken as his own child? Keep reading.

I received a telephone call one day from a young man of whom we had been witnessing to. His wife was a believer and he was seeking the Lord. They had been married for a few years at this particular time. When they got married, he became the stepfather to a pre-teenage boy. What I'm about to share with you is something that I have found to be the norm. In other words, in my experience, this is the way that it happens more times than not. In fact, as a counselor, I have found that married couples usually shy away from counseling when they are having financial problems and even when infidelity has entered into the relationship. However, one thing that brings them to the place of counseling more often than not is friction between the stepfather and the children that he has taken in as if they were his own. And guess what? When there is friction between the good stepfather and his stepchild, the situation can get pretty hostile within the household if the mother fails to, or refuses to take sides with what is right.

So when this young man called me we chitchatted around a little bit and then he said, "Rev., I have a serious problem and I need your input. I need to know whether I am wrong or not." He proceeded to say, "I went into my stepson's room and it was absolutely filthy. So I politely asked him to clean the room." He said the young boy looked at him and went back to what he was doing, totally ignoring his instructions. Needless to say, this didn't set well with the stepfather. So he asked the young boy again to do what he had been asked to do. It was at this point that the young boy responded angrily saying, "You're not my daddy! You can't tell me what to do!" The stepfather said, "When I heard this, I chastised my stepson." He said, "Rev., I lightly chastised him, but the boy flew into a rage screaming, hollering, and even cursing me!"

"Of course, his mother hears all of this and rushes into the room wanting to know what was wrong. So I explained to her exactly what had taken place exposing her son's total disrespect for me. Now Rev., I was already hurt and humiliated by my stepson's disrespectful actions, but when my wife responded angrily by saying, 'You can't spank him! You're not his father!' It was plain to see then that there was an enemy in the household and that enemy was me! Rev., I couldn't believe that my wife would dis' me like that especially in front of her son! Maybe I'm wrong to think that the stepfather is the head of the household just as the biological father would be if he were here. Am I wrong for trying to teach my stepson to be responsible? Am I wrong for disciplining him when and if he decides to rebel? Am I wrong for trying to teach him to submit his childish, selfish will to those good people who are in authority over him? What about it Rev.? Tell me something."

After being placed in the position of answering these three important, poignant questions, there was a silence over the phone about the space of a few seconds. Rev. then proceeded to answer the young man's questions in the following "going here to get there" manner.

Step
'9'
Not Good Enough To Be Their Father

Now earlier I talked about the young male lions that had been forced out of the pride of which they were born into, journeying out in search of a new pride of lions where they could find themselves a lioness to begin mating with. I talked about what usually happens if the female lion had cubs, in that, the male would search them out and kill them. Why? Because, as long as the lioness has cubs that are still at the nursing age, she is not able to mate successfully with the male lion.

Well, somehow it just doesn't seem right for this male lion who has been forced out of his own household, to come in and cause all kinds of trouble in another household of which he has gained admittance into and has been accepted into! I guess one can interpret what the male lion is doing as he kills off his mate's children from her former mate is this: "They are not good enough to be my children!" Even though it doesn't seem right, according to the laws of nature, it is right! Why? Because this is the way that nature has established things and it's impossible for a leopard to change its spots, as it is for a tiger to change its stripes.

Now check this out. What happened in the situation of the stepfather that we just discussed, seems like the reverse of what takes place regularly in the animal kingdom among lions and other non-domestic animals of the wild. The young male lion was kicked to the curb by his own father and was left out in the cold so to speak. However, in many stepfather situations the mother and her child have been kicked to the curb by the biological father of the child. In the case of the young male lion, he came into a situation where he was accepted into another pride, or into the household of another. However, he proceeded to cause a lot of pain and suffering in that household when in our way of thinking, he should have been very appreciative that he had been accepted. There is a similarity here in the case of many stepfathers (like the one who called me), who have married the mother and cared for her child as if he or she was his flesh and blood. In countless cases like this, the mother and the stepchild are the ones who end up turning against her husband and his or her stepfather, causing a lot of pain and suffering in his life! The reality of the matter is this. Seeing that he is a good stepfather just like Mordecai, they should be very appreciative of the exceptional heart of this exceptional man who has chosen to step into a family situation that many men wouldn't dare to tread into.

Now even though it didn't seem right in the case of the young male lion that moved in and destroyed the tranquility of his new family, according to the laws of nature it was right. So how do I answer the young stepfather whose tranquil home had been transformed into a battleground of which he was considered to be the enemy, being pitted against his wife and his stepchild? As far as he was concerned, the declaration of war that was posted up in his home amounted to this: "You're Not Good Enough To Be His Father!"

So we've seen in the case of the young male lion that he operated according to the laws of nature when it came to his lion cub stepchildren, but what about the human stepfather? Has Mother Nature provided him with any kind of insight concerning whether or not he has any authority in his home? Does nature say that stepfathers have the same authority in the home as the biological father if he were there? Or, does he have a lesser authority?

Well fortunately, we don't have to go by the laws of nature concerning this matter of the stepfather and his authority or his lack of authority in the household. So where should we go? As far as Christians are concerned we must go to the architect of the family, who is none other than God the Father. Before we do, let's just look again and see what is the main problem in most households that consist of a mother, her biological child, and a good stepfather. I continue to describe the stepfather as good because there are a whole lot of bad stepfathers who could care less about loving, caring for, and nurturing their stepchild as if he or she were their own. This places them in a category that's opposite that of Mordecai who did these good things for Esther.

Here's the problem. When the good stepfather attempts to correct, to chastise, to instruct, or to discipline his stepchild, many times the stepchild rebels saying, "You're not my father! You can't tell me what to do!" On the same token, many times the mother of the child will say to the good stepfather: "You're not their father! You can't discipline them!"

So first of all, let's point out the hypocrisy and the defective reasoning of the mother and the stepchild. Judging by what both parties are saying, we must conclude that no one in this whole wide world has a right to tell the child what to do other than his or her biological father. Now let's be real. Does the child actually believe this? That's what "You're not my father! You can't tell me what to do!" means. Can this be the underlying reason why so many children have great difficulty with teachers, with employers, and with authority figures as a whole? What about the mother who says, "You're not their father! You can't discipline them?" Does this mean you actually believe that no one in this whole wide world has the right to discipline your child if and when the child does wrong? Mothers, are you teaching your child that the public school system doesn't have the authority to discipline them, and only his or her biological father does? Mothers, are you teaching your child that the law enforcement agencies don't have the authority to discipline your child when he or she break the law? In other words mothers, do you really believe that your child can do as he or she pleases, breaking all the rules that they want to, being highly disrespectful, and nobody has anything to say or do about it? Nobody that is, except his or her biological father? Mothers, what does God the Father, the architect of the family, have to say about the scope of fathers within the home?

> Pro 1:8 My son, hear the instruction of thy father, and forsake not the law of thy mother:
>
> Pro 3:12 For whom the LORD loveth he correcteth; even as a father the son in whom he delighteth.
>
> Pro 4:1 Hear, ye children, the instruction of a father, and attend to know understanding.
>
> Pro 6:20 My son, keep thy father's commandment, and forsake not the law of thy mother:
>
> Pro 10:1 The proverbs of Solomon. A wise son maketh a glad father: but a foolish son is the heaviness of his mother.
>
> Pro 13:1 A wise son heareth his father's instruction: but a scorner heareth not rebuke.
>
> Pro 15:5 A fool despiseth his father's instruction: but he that regardeth reproof is prudent.
>
> Pro 15:20 A wise son maketh a glad father: but a foolish man despiseth his mother.

> Pro 17:21 He that begetteth a fool doeth it to his sorrow: and the father of a fool hath no joy.
>
> Pro 19:13 A foolish son is the calamity of his father: and the contentions of a wife are a continual dropping.
>
> Pro 20:20 Whoso curseth his father or his mother, his lamp shall be put out in obscure darkness.

So according to the Word of God, it is plain that the father has the right in the home to instruct, to correct, to discipline, to chastise, to rebuke, and to restrain. It's also plain that a child who refuses these things will become a fool. A fool who will cause their father to be joyless and their mother to become depressed. Now no doubt someone is thinking that these verses speak only of the father having the right to do these things in the home and they don't say anything about the stepfather having these same rights. Therefore to you, this is proof that the stepfather can never be good enough to be the father of his stepchild. Let's take a look at these beliefs on two levels. First, on the everyday common sense level, then on a scriptural level.

On an everyday common sense level, do we really think that because a man is the biological father of a child, he alone has the ability to instill in the child the things that will enable that child to become an asset to society instead of a liability to society? If this is so, then how can a husband and wife adopt a newborn and proceed to raise that child up in such a noble way that they turn out better than some children who were raised by their biological parents? That is why the various duties of a father that were outlined in the previous verses of scripture are meant to teach a child to submit their naturally selfish will to the will of those in authority over them beginning with the authority figures in their home. Why is this so important to the child? Answer: When they get old enough to begin living as part of the real world, they will not be able to function acceptably if they refuse to listen and conform to first of all, the authority in their own home. Even though biological fathers teaching and training their child is usually the ideal way, they are not the only ones who can teach and train that child to do these things. Would you like to know who else has the capacity to do these things? Other father figures such as teachers, those in mentoring programs, scout leaders, athletic coaches, and leaders in the church. Since this is so, why do we teach children that because a stepfather is not their biological father he cannot instruct them or chastise them in a right way? Here is the common sense bottom line. Basically speaking, even though the primary responsibility falls on the biological parents, any responsible person can accomplish these things. By responsible I mean someone who is mature, loving, caring, and very concerned about the welfare of the child. I'm talking about someone who is willing to commit and dedicate all of their resources long term to accomplish these things. Those of us here on planet Earth can thank God because as important as they are, biological fathers don't have a monopoly in these areas when it comes to correctly raising children. So please hear me mothers and stepchildren. When a child is taught that no one has the right to instruct, to correct, and to discipline him or her except their biological father, this can be one of the most devastating things that they can believe! If you want to short-circuit not only your child's present, but his or her future also, just adhere to and teach them this false belief.

An uncle of mine spoke these words and I tend to agree with him: "Anybody in their right mind wants to go to heaven. In fact, anybody who's out of their right mind wants to go to heaven too!" I said that to say this: "Any mother in her right mind should know better than to teach her children that only their biological father has the right to shape and mold their lives in a productive way. In fact, any mother who is not in her right mind knows better than to teach her children that only their biological father has the right to shape and mold their lives in a productive way too!"

So it is not good old common sense for a mother to boldly declare that her children's good stepfather is not qualified to instruct them and to train them in the same good way that their biological father can.

As we look at it from a scriptural point of view, we will illustrate the general way that the Bible uses the word "father". In other words, if each time the word "father" is used in scripture it's speaking about the biological father and him only, then we will have to concur with those mothers who more or less say to their husband concerning his stepchildren, "You're not good enough to be their father. That is why you need to forget about trying to tell them what to do and about trying to discipline them!"

1Ki 15:1 Now in the eighteenth year of king Jeroboam the son of Nebat reigned Abijam over Judah.

1Ki 15:2 Three years reigned he in Jerusalem. And his mother's name was Maachah, the daughter of Abishalom.

1Ki 15:3 And he walked in all the sins of his father, which he had done before him: and his heart was not perfect with the LORD his God, as the heart of David his father.

At verse 3, we see that King Jeroboam was a very sinful man who committed the same sins that his father committed before him. The latter part of that same verse says King Jeroboam's heart was not perfect before the Lord as the heart of David his father. So within the same verse, we see that King Jeroboam's father was mentioned twice. We're told that he had an evil heart exactly as his father did. Then it says that King Jeroboam's heart was not perfect towards God as the heart of his father David's was. So how many fathers did Jeroboam have? Answer: Like you and I, Jeroboam had only one biological father. This is the one referred to as being evil. Why then, does verse 3 call David his father also? Why? Because David was a great-grandfather of Jeroboam several generations before Jeroboam was even born. You will find that the way father is used here is consistent throughout the Word of God. The word "father" not only refers to biological fathers, but also to grandfathers even several generations back. At 2 Kings 18 we see the same thing spoken concerning Hezekiah and his fathers:

> 2Ki 18:1 Now it came to pass in the third year of Hoshea son of Elah king of Israel, that Hezekiah the son of Ahaz king of Judah began to reign.
>
> 2Ki 18:2 Twenty and five years old was he when he began to reign; and he reigned twenty and nine years in Jerusalem. His mother's name also was Abi, the daughter of Zachariah.
>
> 2Ki 18:3 And he did that which was right in the sight of the LORD, according to all that David his father did.

At verse 1 we're told that Hezekiah's father was Ahaz. Then at verse 3 David is mentioned as Hezekiah's father also. What's interesting here is that David is called Hezekiah's father even though David lived about 300 years before Hezekiah! What we can't afford to miss here is this: We understand and accept without hesitation the fact that we can inherit physical characteristics from our ancestors. Healthy parents pass on healthy bodies to their offspring. The same is true in the spiritual realm. The righteous ways of a father can be passed down through many generations. The same is true of fathers who live unrighteous lives. We inherit and we turn around and pass on what we have inherited. So contrary to the popular beliefs of many organizations in our day and time, fathers are important! Fathers are needed!

And guess what? I'm not talking specifically about and only about biological fathers. But rather, I'm referring to all men who stand in the position of the father. And this most definitely, by all means, without a shadow of a doubt, includes good stepfathers. In fact, outside of the biological father, the stepfather is the one who can have the most profound affect in the life of his stepchild more so than any other father figure. Why? Because the stepfather is the husband of his stepchild's mother and he lives in the same household with them. This equates into a daily teaching atmosphere where husband and wife can work together to *"Train up the child in the way that he should go and when he is old he will not depart from it"* (Pro 22:6). This is why good stepfathers are so special in God's sight. This is also why Satan desires to short-circuit the positive affect that good stepfathers can have in a family setting that for whatever reasons, consists of only a mother and her child. No, the good stepfather is not the biological father. No, the good stepfather can never become the biological father. No, the good stepfather can never pass on physical traits to his stepchild. In this respect, I guess we can say that he isn't good enough. Nevertheless, there are some things that he is more than good enough for. He can step in and instill righteousness into his stepchild that will be passed down generation after generation after generation after generation. Maybe that is why stepfathers are called stepfathers.

While all of this is good, we are constantly bombarded with reports about the abuse in households by a lot of bad stepfathers who could care less about being the type of father to their stepchild as the good man Mordecai was to Esther. The purpose of this book is to give honor to whom honor is due, and respect to whom respect is due. I believe that the good stepfather has been basically kicked to the curb along with the hordes of bad ones and isn't even close to receiving the honor and the respect that's due him.

Now in case you are wondering what constitutes a good stepfather, let me just give you a few basic characteristics:

1. Good stepfathers are determined to love their wives and their stepchildren with an unconditional love. In order to accomplish this, especially concerning the stepchildren, good stepfathers realize that there will be extraordinary trials and tribulations that he must successfully overcome.

2. Good stepfathers know that time and great patience must be exercised on their part. There can be many roadblocks and stumbling blocks that materialize between the stepchild and the stepfather that must be overcome before a healthy, mutual, respectful relationship can be formed. The younger the child, the less time and patience it will usually take, but the opposite is usually true the older the child is.

3. Good stepfathers are determined to handle rejection without becoming bitter and falling victim to retaliation. Patience is a great virtue that enables the good stepfather to allow his stepchild to advance in the relationship at his or her own pace, and not give up when and if the child rejects him.

4.   A good stepfather realizes that his wife is his greatest asset in the development of a very livable atmosphere within the home. Therefore, in the beginning, he will allow the mother to handle most of the disciplining in the household while he works at establishing a trusting relationship with the child. At the same time, it is a must that he is able to recognize when the child is attempting to manipulate him and his wife against each other.

5.   Good stepfathers do not allow themselves to become their stepchild's best friend at the expense of not becoming an authority figure in their lives. Whenever you hear a parent saying, "My child and I are best friends," you are listening to a parent who has failed to establish the right kind of authoritative parent-child relationship with their child.

6.   Good stepfathers are very careful not to overreact when they think that the biological mother, his wife, is too lenient with her child. Even though being too lenient can be detrimental, so can being too strict on his part.

This is by no means an exhaustive list, but it can be used in order to begin establishing a great foundation within the confines of the home that includes a stepparent, whether they are male or female. Needless to say, this would be an answer to prayer if all stepfathers operated in this good way within the household, but realistically this is not the case in far too many stepfather households. That's why my aim was to bring attention to the good stepfathers who are attempting to do all of these good things and more, but are being treated like the enemy not only by his stepchild, but also by his spouse who is the child's biological mother.

So please realize that it hurts God to His heart when a good stepfather hears these cold, sharp, dehumanizing words coming from his stepchild and his wife: "You can't tell me what to do! You're not my father!" "You can't discipline them! You're not their father!" Why are the stepchildren (with the support of their mother), saying that the good stepfather cannot chastise them or tell them what to do? Why? Well in their opinion, he is not good enough to be their father.

Step
'10'
He's Good, But Not Good Enough

I'd like to drop a little more common sense on you concerning something that is highly accepted and praised worldwide because it fills a great need, and saves those of us who inhabit planet Earth's untold expense. The world that we live in today is filled with countless great and very purposeful inventions. The world is literally full of them. That's why all of us are deeply indebted to inventors. Why? Because, they have given us the highly technological way of life that we are so accustomed to.

But there is one group that if not for them, our lifestyles would cease to be what they are now regardless of these great inventions. This aggregate of people worldwide is busy everyday manufacturing replacement parts. Oh yeah, we need to really thank God for replacement parts. I mean we really need to thank God that our great need for replacement parts is being fulfilled! In case you may not realize why we need replacement parts, check this out:

> Gen 3:17 And unto Adam he said, Because thou hast hearkened unto the voice of thy wife, and hast eaten of the tree, of which I commanded thee, saying, Thou shalt not eat of it: cursed is the ground for thy sake; in sorrow shalt thou eat of it all the days of thy life;

> Gen 3:18 Thorns also and thistles shall it bring forth to thee; and thou shalt eat the herb of the field;

> Gen 3:19 In the sweat of thy face shalt thou eat bread, till thou return unto the ground; for out of it wast thou taken: for dust thou art, and unto dust shalt thou return.

Here in Genesis chapter three, we see God holding court in the Garden of Eden. It is there that He pronounces various judgments upon all those who were involved in the fall of man. It is there within these judgements that we find the answer to the question: "Why do we need replacement parts?"

I'd like for you to take notice of these words in verse 17: *"...cursed is the ground for thy sake."* So Adam is the one responsible for our needing replacement parts! Why? Because God said, *"Because of your sin Adam, the earth, or the ground is cursed"* (paraphrased). I'm sure that some of you are probably scratching your head right about now saying, "Huh?" O.K., are you through scratching? Brush the spiritual dandruff off and listen to this. As we look around, we would be very hard pressed to find anything that we use on an everyday basis that didn't originally come out of the ground. For example, the concrete, the metal, the plastic, the wood, the glass, the paper, and all of the different variations of these things were created from materials that came out of the ground. A ground, that happens to be a cursed ground. How many of you know that if not for this cursed ground, everything coming out of it would last forever without aging?

The cursed ground is why everything wears out and wears down. I painted my house with some quality paint a few years ago, but the paint has since faded. Even though I try to ignore it, my honey do list is a constant reminder that the house needs repainting. Thanks a lot Adam! When you go to purchase new tires for your new automobile because the original ones are worn down, you can thank Adam for it! When your uncle in Washington, D.C. calls for an audit of your business, and you pull out your old records with unreadable, faded ink, you can blame it on Adam! And guess what? The reason why we as humans wear out and wear down is because we too were created from this cursed ground. Out of the earth we came and to the earth we will return. This of course speaks of our physical bodies because our spirit and soul are immortal and will spend the rest of eternity in heaven or in hell. That's right! Once a person is born into this world, he or she will end up in heaven or hell dependent upon whether or not they live this life in the here and now according to the will of God or not. Eternal thanks Adam! Now before we get to hating on Adam, here is some good news about something that he passed on that is a great blessing to all of us who live on planet Earth:

> Gen 2:18 And the LORD God said, It is not good that the man should be alone; I will make him an help meet for him.

> Gen 2:19 And out of the ground the LORD God formed every beast of the field, and every fowl of the air; and brought them unto Adam to see what he would call them: and whatsoever Adam called every living creature, that was the name thereof.

> Gen 2:20 And Adam gave names to all cattle, and to the fowl of the air, and to every beast of the field; but for Adam there was not found an help meet for him.

> Gen 2:21 And the LORD God caused a deep sleep to fall upon Adam, and he slept: and he took one of his ribs, and closed up the flesh instead thereof;

> Gen 2:22 And the rib, which the LORD God had taken from man, made he a woman, and brought her unto the man.

> Gen 2:23 And Adam said, This is now bone of my bones, and flesh of my flesh: she shall be called Woman, because she was taken out of Man.

> Gen 2:24 Therefore shall a man leave his father and his mother, and shall cleave unto his wife: and they shall be one flesh.

So we see here that after God finished creating all the living creatures in the earth, Adam named all of them! Verse 19 tells us, *"Whatsoever Adam called every living creature, that was their name thereof."* People, Adam had to be one smart man! Why? Because I'm absolutely sure that the smartest man in the world today would have given out of names long before the task was finished of naming every living creature that God had created. Are you with me?

Believe it or not, Adam was next to God. Before the fall, he was higher than the angels. The man was so smart that even after thousands of years with a fallen sin nature, man is still fairly smart today! And woman is even smarter (I had to say that on behalf of my wife)! So even though Adam was the cause of the ground being cursed (which causes every thing that comes out of the ground to wear out and to wear down), we can't go around hating on Adam. Why not? Because Adam passed down intelligence to us. That's why we need to give Adam his props. Why should we thank God for Adam? Because somebody used that inherited intelligence to see the great need for replacements parts! Here is an excellent example that reveals just how important replacement parts are. In the state that I live the law requires that a cracked automobile front windshield be replaced. Let's just suppose that there were no replacement windshields. We would either have to stop driving the car, or buy a new car with a good windshield. In the same sense, suppose there were no replacement tires for that same automobile. The whole car would be useless simply because there would be no such thing as replacement tires! Disposable cameras are right on, but disposable cars? I don't think so!

What about computers? Suppose we buy a new computer for $2000, but after a while the video card goes bad. Without the video card we cannot see anything on the monitor. A replacement video card can be purchased for about $15. We could drop it in and before we know it we will be computing right along as before. Assuming of course, that someone somewhere has invented replacement video cards! If not, then we would either have to forget about using the computer and revert back to the Stone Age, or we would have to spend a fresh $2000 for another computer. Can we see the utmost importance of replacement parts? The inventions are great, but if there were no replacement parts for these millions of inventions, we would be in a world of trouble.

I need to make one last important point that applies to practically all replacements parts. When we set out to purchase replacement parts, we can usually get original equipment replacement parts from the company that manufactured the part. These original equipment replacement parts usually cost more than the slew of other replacement parts that we can purchase from various other sources that produces after market replacement parts. Now even though there are different sources for these replacement parts, all of them must meet a minimum set of specifications before they can be sold to the public. In fact, many times we can purchase replacement parts with specifications that are higher than those of the original factory parts! In other words, they last longer and are better than the original factory parts that came on the equipment! So when it comes to replacement parts, we can rest assured that man is so intelligent that the parts are not only good, but they can be more than good. Highlight this, please. The man-made replacement part can be of a better quality and provide more longevity than the factory original part.

So what has all of this to do with good stepfathers? I'm glad you asked. Let me answer that question like this. In many households where the good stepfather has been reduced to the enemy of his stepchild and his or her mother, it seems as though this is the case: Stepfather, you're good, but you're not good enough to replace the original (the biological father).

Now as I compare replacement parts with replacement fathers, it is most definitely not my intention to relegate a human being down to the position of a mechanized replacement part. It's only in a general way that I'm doing this, with the hope of enabling us to see the irony of the position of far too many stepchildren and their mothers concerning their husband and their good stepfather. It is my hope, that they will recognize what they are actually saying when they say that a man created in the image of God Himself, cannot find a way to effectively replace another man if that man who needs replacing is the original father. However, these same individuals believe that when it comes to replacing a lifeless, brainless, mechanical part that is broken or mal-functioning, another lifeless, brainless, man-made, mechanical replacement part can do a better job than the original factory part!

The Lord has blessed me to do some song writing when time permits. The title of a song that I recently wrote is called, "Simple and Plain." These are the words to the chorus: "Simple and plain! Can you hear what I'm saying? If you can't understand this Gospel, then you must be insane!" I know, it's kind of radical, but somebody has to do it, so it might as well be me. I went where I just went because of where I went in the preceding paragraph. I need to say again what I said then, in order to make sure that it's "Simple and plain! Can you hear what I'm saying?"

So here it is, as simple and plain as I can make it. It doesn't make sense when a person believes that a man-made replacement part can be acceptable or even better than the man-made original part, but at the same time believe that a stepfather, who is made in the image of God, is not acceptable and most definitely cannot be better than the original father who is not performing as a good father should! Now I know that this is a "run on sentence," but please overlook it because I had to run with it in an attempt to make it "Simple and plain! Can you hear what I'm saying?"

This is the irony of this whole matter of the good stepfather not being good enough to step in and effectively do what the biological father is not doing. Why can't the good stepfather effectively replace the defective biological father? Well, if you listen to the mother and the stepchild, it's "simple and plain, if we can hear what they're saying." To them, the good stepfather just cannot meet the specifications of true fatherhood! It is my prayer that we can't hear what they are saying! Why? Because most statistics show that the majority of families where stepfathers are present are the result of deadbeat, biological fathers who deserted their wife and children, or the result of children born out of wedlock where a marriage never took place between their mother and the children's biological father. So when the good stepfather steps in and loves his wife and his stepchild with an unconditional love, the good stepfather in his replacement role, is actually doing something better than what the biological father is doing! What makes the good stepfather's actions even the more noble is the fact that he is doing these things while being exposed to more stress, more duress, and more pressure than the biological father would be exposed to if he stuck around and became a good father.

It's sort of O.K. for children to grow up believing in something harmless that is not true, like Santa Claus, but stepchildren should not grow up with the erroneous belief that bad biological fathers are better than good stepfathers! But yet and still, the good stepfather is looked upon as an inferior, below specifications product who is good enough to be a stepfather, but he's not good enough to replace the good things that the biological father is not bringing about in the family setting. In the eyes of certain unappreciative stepchildren and their unappreciative mothers, the good stepfather is good enough to go out and work through blood, sweat and tears and bring his paycheck home to them. He's good enough to spend quality time with the children by taking them to and picking them up from after school activities, the movies, and everywhere else. To the mother, he's good enough to be her husband. He's good enough for her to trust in his fidelity as she intimately shares her bed with him. In their eyes, even though he's good enough, he's not good enough! That's what, "You can't tell me what to do! You're not my father!" means. That's what, "You can't discipline them! You're not their father!" means. On the one hand, when it comes to man-made replacement parts, that same mother and stepchild will wholeheartedly agree that they're good, and many are able to be better than the original parts. While on the other hand, when it comes to the good stepfather, they wholeheartedly agree that he's good enough for some things, but there is no way that he can be good enough to replace the biological father. This is the way that it is regardless of the fact that he is doing lots of good things that the biological father failed to do, refused to do, didn't do, couldn't do, wouldn't do, or can't do! Yet and still, he is just not good enough! God told me to make it so that you could take it, but I can't make it any better than that. I can't tiptoe through the tulips on this one.

You see, these cold, sharp, bitter, hurtful words and non-beatitude attitudes are never directed towards biological fathers. The biological father doesn't have to worry about hearing his child say, "You can't tell me what to do! You're not my father!" The biological father doesn't have to worry about hearing his wife say, "You can't discipline them! You're not their father!" Amen? I'm just wondering if this thing is "Simple and plain? Can you hear what I'm saying?"

Let's sum it all up by saying, it looks like the good stepfather is good enough as long as he doesn't step outside of his boundaries, which some believe that he does when he attempts to discipline, chastise, or instruct his stepchild. As long as the good stepfather doesn't step outside of these boundaries, it seems as though the mother and the stepchild are willing to play the part of good and loving wife, and good and loving stepchild. However, if and when he does step outside of these boundaries, he's through being good enough to be the husband. He's through being good enough to be the stepfather and he now becomes "not their father and not my father." So good stepfather, their advice seems to be: Don't step outside of these boundaries! Maybe that's why some people call a stepfather a stepfather.

To everyone who has an ear to hear, please hear me now. God wants us to be aware of the way that He regards and values good stepfathers. I believe that God wants us to realize that when we compare the love of a biological father to that of a good stepfather, the love of the good stepfather has to be an exceptional love that must make exceptional sacrifices. I'm talking about the kind of love and sacrifice which enables him to weather the unique storms in an exceptional family situation without giving up, giving out, or giving in. Without hating but relating, not falling into depression, but always making an indelible impression.

Our realization of how God values good stepfathers is of utmost importance because like it or not, stepparent families are here to stay. A small percentage come about as a result of the death of the biological father, while most probably come about because of deadbeat fathers who desert their families. Some also come about as a result of broken marriages and relationships.

I read a joke once where a little girl said to her mother: "Mama, since the stork brings babies, and Santa brings toys, and God is our Father, what do we need daddy for?" Even though it's kind of funny, realistically it represents the mindset of far too many people in our society today. Since God established the father as the head of the family, Satan has set out to get rid of the father. If he can lose the father, it's easier for him to misuse the mother, and then abuse the children.

That is why some children who grow up without the presence of their biological father are very fortunate to have good stepfathers who help to fill the empty place and provide the other half of parental guidance that enables the family to function in a more normal and productive way. Unless of course, they along with their mother become guilty of muzzling the (good stepfather) ox who is treading their corn.

Step

'11'

Examining The Heart Of God

R-E-S-P-E-C-T

"So God created man in his own image, in the image of God created he him; male and female created he them" (Genesis 1:27). The word genesis means beginning. In the beginning of the Bible we see the basis for humankind to be treated with the utmost respect regardless of race, creed, color, or national origin. In case you missed it, here is the reason again: Every human being reflects the nature of God, which means we are Godlike as opposed to animal like. Take that, evolutionists!

It is obvious that throughout the ages mankind has continued to disregard the sacred dignity of their fellow man that God has placed upon every human being. This is why history is replete with incident after incident of the extreme violation of human rights worldwide. In fact, many times those who get the most honor and respect among men are the ones who blatantly disregard the honor and respect that God has placed upon mankind! For instance, the honor and respect that God has placed upon a woman has been degraded down to that of female dogs (bitches), and a tool that you dig in the ground with (hoes)! And the ones mainly involved in this degradation are being paid millions of dollars to do it by the music industry.

The sanctity of human life has deteriorated to the point that we are a part of a society that has also almost totally ignored the God ordained sacredness of human life and valued it to be less than that of animals! Buckle your seatbelts now people because we don't want anybody to fall out! To the dismay of only a few, the life of many animals has been given more value than human lives to the point that a person can be fined and locked down if they kill a baby eagle that's inside of its mother's egg waiting to be born. While at the same time, a person can be paid good money and praised when they kill a baby human that's inside of his or her mother's womb waiting to be born! What a total lack of dignity and respect for another human being!

It is no wonder that when it comes to a good stepfather, there seems to be no hesitation to take away from him the same dignity and respect that God has placed upon all of mankind. We need to know that when we look at the heart of God, it is obvious that this is not the way that it was meant to be from the genesis. If we examine the heart of God from the beginning, it will be clear that He purposed for all of mankind, male and female, to be showered with R-E-S-P-E-C-T! That's right, Aretha Franklin hit the nail dead on the head when she sang about R-E-S-P-E-C-T!

I would like to call your attention to one particular way that's acceptable on a large scale throughout this society of ours when it comes to respecting the dignity of humankind. Now what I'm about to share here may seem like something that is trivial. It may seem like something that is of little significance, and of little substance. The good stepfather himself may even think that it is not a large enough matter to even consider, even though it is meant to uplift and encourage him. Even though some good stepfathers may feel this way, I am simply endeavoring to show you the heart of God. So, if I can show you the heart of God, then there is a very good chance that regardless of what some good stepfathers might say, more than likely, it just may be something that they would like to receive. What I'm talking about is R-E-S-P-E-C-T!

In our society, many things that deal with the respect and dignity of humankind has deteriorated over the years like the walls of the Grand Canyon. Nevertheless, there is one thing that is still pretty much intact when it comes to addressing "grown folk" (as the old folk used to call adults). Years ago, it was automatic for those younger to address adults with the terms Sir and Ma'am. It was Yes Sir, No Sir, Yes Ma'am, or No Ma'am. Now even though a simple yes or no was acceptable, adding the title of Sir or Ma'am seemed to confer more honor, respect and value upon the individual being addressed.

Another acceptable way that was, and still is, quite common that places honor, respect and value upon adults is to address them as "Mr. or Mrs." These honorable terms can be used to preface a person's first or last name. In other words, to address me as Mr. James or as Mr. McCormick has the same honorable effect.

When I was growing up in the 50's and 60's, I believe that young people in general respected grown people a whole lot more than today as far as how we addressed our elders. This was ingrained so deep within us that right now today, the vast majority of young people who has some semblance of home training still dare not disrespect someone who is their elder by addressing them only by their first name. Unless of course, you just happen to be a stepfather. It is then that all of the respect and honor that a person of his statue deserves is usually thrown out of the window and trampled under the foot of men.

Hear me now people. God told me to make it so that you could take it. I'll do my best on this one. Here we have children who respectfully address their teachers by calling them Mr. or Mrs., or even Miss so and so. They respectfully address their principal in like manner by calling him or her Principal so in so. They respectfully address their coaches by placing Coach before their first or last name. In the church environment they respectfully address the head of the church by calling him or her Pastor so and so.

So what is it about a stepfather that causes all of this society-wide respect and honor to vanish?

Why is it that you can hear a child disrespectfully addressing his or her stepfather by referring to him as James, Robert, John, etc.? The biological father would probably think that his child was demon possessed if he or she approached him and called him by his first name! He will probably put his hand over his heart like Fred Sanford used to do and stumble backwards as if to have a heart attack because of the shock of hearing what he just heard! The mother would quickly and vehemently protest and so would the biological father. In fact, people outside of the family would intervene and try to talk some sense into the disrespectful child. Why? Because in our society it still isn't acceptable by a long shot for a child to disrespect an adult by addressing them by their first name only. Unless of course, you just happen to be a stepfather. It is then that something that's so unacceptable in the eyes of society now becomes A.O.K. So among all of the things that a good stepfather has to go through and to put up with that the biological father doesn't, it seems to be quite the norm for him to be stripped of the respect and the honor that is automatic to everybody else.

As I say this, I'm well aware of and very sensitive to the fact that in a household with a stepfather, the stepchildren can be torn with various strong emotions, like that of trying to figure out how they should address their stepfather. If they call him father, they may feel that they are dishonoring their biological father. This can be especially so in the case of a divorce and they are still strongly attached to their biological father. This problem can be more intense depending upon the age of the children. But one thing is for sure, instead of calling the man, "Hey Joe! Or "Hey James! Or hey any first name, since you do acknowledge him as your stepfather, why not just call him "Stepfather"? It is my opinion that to be addressed as Stepfather can bring more honor and respect than to be called father! I say this because more and more, people are realizing that it takes a special kind of man with a special heart of love to step into a family situation where the pressure on him will be extraordinary, and then proceed to do an excellent job!

That is why I believe that if we examine the heart of God closely, we will find that God honors it when the mother makes sure that her underage children honor her husband and their stepfather by addressing him respectfully. Either as father, stepfather, or in a way that gives him the honor and respect that is due to him because of the capacity that he is in. Well, let's see if we can use scripture to locate the heart of God on this matter of how someone in the capacity of father should be addressed, whether he be the biological father or the stepfather.

> Joh 3:16   For God so loved the world, that he gave his only begotten Son, that whosoever believeth in him should not perish, but have everlasting life.
>
> 2Co 6:17 Wherefore come out from among them, and be ye separate, saith the Lord, and touch not the unclean thing; and I will receive you,
>
> 2Co 6:18 And will be a Father unto you, and ye shall be my sons and daughters, saith the Lord Almighty.

So we see here that God engendered only one son. Christ is God's only engendered son. But then we see at 2 Corinthians 6 that God speaks about other sons and daughters of His. Who are these other sons and daughters of God of whom He did not engender as He did Christ? Answer: They are everyone who has accepted Jesus as their Lord and Savior. God said, "When you or I or any person accepts His Son Jesus as their personal Lord and Savior, He will be a Father to us." So in the broad sense of it all, God is a Stepfather to every born again believer! So as far as the heart of God (our Stepfather) is concerned, how does God want us to address Him?

> Mat 6:8   Be not ye therefore like unto them: for your Father knoweth what things ye have need of, before ye ask him.
>
> Mat 6:9   After this manner therefore pray ye: Our Father which art in heaven, Hallowed be thy name.
>
> Gal 4:4 But when the fulness of the time was come, God sent forth his Son, made of a woman, made under the law,
>
> Gal 4:5   To redeem them that were under the law, that we might receive the adoption of sons.
>
> Gal 4:6 And because ye are sons, God hath sent forth the Spirit of his Son into your hearts, crying, Abba, Father.

So we see here at Matthew 6 that God, who has taken us in as if we were His own(ly) begotten children, God wants us to address Him as Father. Then, at Galatians 4 we're told that proof of our sonship comes in the form of the Spirit of Christ entering into our hearts and moving us to address God as "Abba, Father". Abba itself means father. The Spirit of Christ, the only begotten of God, desires for us to address His Father God and our Father God as "Father, Father."

Let me reiterate this again. What I'm attempting to show you is the heart of God. I am not implying that someone is in sin if they fail to address stepfathers in respect to the role that they're actually occupying. So let's continue to examine the heart of God.

As we know, there are countless situations today where a mother is stuck with the responsibility of rearing her child without any support whatsoever from the biological father even though he is still alive and well and able to provide support. Many of these mothers remarry or marry for the first time and the stepfather enters into the household. Sad to say, a great number of these stepfathers are not like Mordecai. In fact, a great number of these stepfathers aren't any better than the biological father who cared nothing for his children and walked out on them. To break it on down, I stand to believe that many of these bad stepfathers are the same ones who had already deserted their own biological children and left them to fend for themselves the best that they could. And guess what? These bad stepfathers not only mistreat and sometimes abuse their stepchild, but many times their new wife gives birth from them and they become a biological father again in the same house where they are currently filling the role being of a bad stepfather! So now he's up and out of there in search of another place to lay his head. He's in search of another willing bed, and as far as his newest set of biological children are concerned, he might as well be dead! What I'm saying is, even though his children are hoping and praying that he would start to live in circumspect, discontinue his neglect, and try to show some respect, he could care less! Hello somebody!

Now even though they are rare, some of these mothers end up with a husband who is a good stepfather. So let's say the mother has one or more underage children and the stepfather wants to adopt them. This is a step that most will not take. Why? Because by doing so, the stepfather now becomes legally responsible for the children as if they were his own biological children. In most cases where there has been a divorce between their mother and their biological father, the children bear the last name of their biological father. So when the stepfather shows forth this exceptional love for his stepchildren and adopts them, which makes him morally and legally responsible for them, what think ye? Should the children's last name be changed to his last name? Now as I said earlier, the above average good stepfather may say that it makes no difference one way or the other to them. They may even feel like I am being overly concerned with trivialities. Nevertheless, as I said, all that I'm trying to do is to show you the heart of God our Father in these matters with the hope that we can see how God loves and values a good stepfather.

So we have seen that when God adopts us as believers into His family, he wants us to address Him as Father. We saw that, right? We now need to discover the heart of God as far as our taking on His name is concerned.

> Rev 3:8 I know thy works: behold, I have set before thee an open door, and no man can shut it: for thou hast a little strength, and hast kept my word, and hast not denied my name.
>
> Rev 3:12 Him that overcometh will I make a pillar in the temple of my God, and he shall go no more out: and I will write upon him the name of my God, and the name of the city of my God, which is new Jerusalem, which cometh down out of heaven from my God: and I will write upon him my new name.

In verse 8, we see that God seems to be proud of His children who among other things, kept His word and did not deny His name. Then at verse 12, it is clear that God's desire is for those who belong to Him to be known and recognized as belonging to Him. How? By bearing His name. In essence, this is what it looks like. Since God is paying the cost to be the boss, He deserves and demands the R-E-S-P-E-C-T and the honor that comes along with it. Since you are my child, bear my name. Since I stepped in and rescued you from a life of sin and degradation, bear my name. Since I have taken on the total responsibility for your care and your protection, bear my name. This seems to be the heart of God.

Now on the everyday natural side of things, this is something that we practice 24 & 7. My wife and I have owned several cars over the years, but it wasn't until the year 2002 that we purchased our first brand new car. Up until then we always purchased a pre-owned car. Pre-owned means it used to belong to somebody else and was registered in their name. Flow with me now people because I'm just trying to make it "Simple and plain. Can you hear what I'm saying?" So when we went to the current owner and met their demands for payment, the pre-owned car became our car. And guess what? The first thing that we did was to get the car transferred out of the name of the previous owner and into our name. Why? Because the car now belonged to us regardless of who used to own it. What I'm saying is, since we are now responsible for the tag registration, the insurance, and the maintenance of it, put it in our name. Take their personalized tag off the front of it and put ours on it! Simple and plain, we wouldn't have it any other way. Can you hear what I'm saying?

The same is true when we go to purchase a pre-owned house from a seller. It makes no difference whose name it is in, unless of course, the owner is Beelzebub! If this was the case and we didn't believe in casting out demons, it may make a difference! Otherwise, under most circumstances, it makes no difference whose name is currently on the deed to the house, but what makes all the difference in the world is whose name is on the deed after we purchase it. Why? Because the one whose name was previously on the deed is no longer responsible for paying for it nor are they any longer responsible for the upkeep of it, we are. We demand that our name be placed on the things that we own because a name shows who has authority over what! "In the name of Jesus" doesn't mean the literal name of Jesus, but rather, it means by the authority of Jesus! So these are some things that a mother and her child can at least consider concerning her husband and his or her good stepfather, even if he says it doesn't matter. What else can we expect him to say? He's just a good man! It can never hurt to just consider things that say to him, "you are an exceptional man with an exceptional heart of love and compassion. We, in like manner, love you with the same love and tenderness. This is why you can rest assured that you have our utmost R-E-S-P-E-C-T!"

Step
'12'
Give Stepfathers Their Props

Exo 2:5 And the daughter of Pharaoh came down to wash *herself* at the river; and her maidens walked along by the river's side; and when she saw the ark among the flags, she sent her maid to fetch it.

Exo 2:6 And when she had opened *it*, she saw the child: and, behold, the babe wept. And she had compassion on him, and said, This *is one* of the Hebrews' children.

Exo 2:7 Then said his sister to Pharaoh's daughter, Shall I go and call to thee a nurse of the Hebrew women, that she may nurse the child for thee?

Exo 2:8 And Pharaoh's daughter said to her, Go. And the maid went and called the child's mother.

Exo 2:9 And Pharaoh's daughter said unto her, Take this child away, and nurse it for

> me, and I will give *thee* thy wages. And
> the woman took the child, and nursed it.
>
> Exo 2:10   And the child grew, and she
> brought him unto Pharaoh's daughter, and
> he became her son. And she called his
> name Moses: and she said, Because I drew
> him out of the water.

When we consider the Old Testament and all of its true life characters, if we had the task of choosing one from among them as the greatest, I believe that Moses would probably be the unanimous choice. In fact, Moses is mentioned close to 100 times in the New Testament while the other Old Testament prophets are rarely mentioned. What's interesting is, as we look at the scriptural account of the life of Moses we see that the daughter of Pharaoh adopted him, which probably made Pharaoh the main male figure in Moses' life and not his biological father. Looking at what Moses went on to accomplish in life let's us know that someone other than Moses' biological father must have raised him up pretty good. I don't know, but if we listen closely we may hear God saying: "Stepfathers can be good enough!"

> Mat 1:18   Now the birth of Jesus Christ
> was on this wise: When as his mother Mary
> was espoused to Joseph, before they came
> together, she was found with child of the
> Holy Ghost.
>
> Mat 1:19 Then Joseph her husband, being
> a just *man*, and not willing to make her a
> publick example, was minded to put her
> away privily.

Mat 1:20 But while he thought on these things, behold, the angel of the Lord appeared unto him in a dream, saying, Joseph, thou son of David, fear not to take unto thee Mary thy wife: for that which is conceived in her is of the Holy Ghost.

Mat 1:21 And she shall bring forth a son, and thou shalt call his name JESUS: for he shall save his people from their sins.

Mat 1:22 Now all this was done, that it might be fulfilled which was spoken of the Lord by the prophet, saying,

Mat 1:23 Behold, a virgin shall be with child, and shall bring forth a son, and they shall call his name Emmanuel, which being interpreted is, God with us.

Mat 1:24 Then Joseph being raised from sleep did as the angel of the Lord had bidden him, and took unto him his wife:

Mat 1:25 And knew her not till she had brought forth her firstborn son: and he called his name JESUS.

When we consider all of the prophets and characters of the New Testament, Jesus the Christ is without a doubt the most important. Why? Because He is Emmanuel! Jesus is God manifested in the flesh! Jesus is God's only begotten son who came to take away the sin of the world!

These select verses of scripture taken from Matthew chapter 1 reveals to us that the virgin Mary became pregnant supernaturally via the Holy Spirit of God. So this means that Joseph was not the biological father of their first son. Now people, you're talking about the great importance of a stepfather in the eyes of God! Here is the Almighty God, trusting the care, the nurturing and the protection of His only begotten son to a stepfather! There was a lot riding on Emmanuel's good stepfather! This is the stepson who would grow up to save the world from sin! I believe that these are two great biblical examples that place God's honor upon the exceptional effort of love and sacrifice of good stepfathers who step into the role of being a father to the fatherless. Maybe that's why stepfathers are called stepfathers and why good stepfathers everywhere should be given their props.

About The Author

It becomes obvious to almost everyone who hears J. F. McCormick, III., ministering that he has a unique anointing. In fact, when he gave his life to Christ twenty one years ago, the call on his life to preach was so strong and unique that seven days later he was licensed as he preached his first sermon at a Youth Day service. He began pastoring six years later at Friendship Full Gospel Church in Lakeland, Florida. The Lord has used him to minister many dynamic messages with dynamic titles and many times with life changing props and illustrations. His desire is to see the family setup and prospering the way that God has ordained that it should.

Printed in the United States
68196LVS00001B/51